365 WAYS
TO
BREATHE

Breathe your way to a happy,
healthy, beautiful life!

365 WAYS TO BREATHE

* * * * *

Breathe your way to a happy,
healthy, beautiful life!

DEBORAH GARLAND

Radiance Publishing

The exercises and practices in this book are not intended to replace the services of your physician, or to provide an alternative to professional medical treatment. *365 Ways To Breathe* offers no diagnosis of, or treatment, for any specific medical problem that you may have. Practices and inspirations are given solely for educational purposes - either to explore the possible relationship of breathing to health, or to expose the reader to insights about health and well being. The breathing practices outlined here are gentle, and should - if carried out as described - be beneficial to overall physical and psychological health. If you have any serious medical or psychological problems, such as: heart disease, high blood pressure, cancer, mental illness, recent surgeries, or any other medical condition; you should consult your physician before practicing any of the exercises described here.

Cover Design by Deborah Garland
Illustrations and Book Design by Deborah Garland

Library of Congress Control Number: 2016946238

ISBN 978-0-692-74996-8

for my mittra

We begin our life with a single breath, and that's also how we leave. Breathing is natural and instinctual, and has the power to transform our lives – breath by breath.

Breath infuses every cell and every atom in our body with vital life force. We can harness the life force within our breath to create more energy, lift our mood, calm ourselves down, balance our emotions, eliminate stress, create vibrant health, radiate with glowing beauty, access higher realms of spirituality, sharpen concentration, become more confident... and the list goes on and on. What other technique provides all of that - and is free, requires no equipment, can be done anywhere and anytime, and you already know how to do it!

This book truly can benefit each and every one of us. It is filled with easy and quick techniques and inspirations to help you breathe your way to a healthier, happier, more radiant life. There is no right or wrong way to read through it. Maybe keep a copy on your nightstand and select a breath you'd like to try that day. Or have a copy in your office or reception area for customers and colleagues to discover. Or open a meeting with one of the inspirational quotes and do a breathing exercise together. Or share with a loved one or yourself when times are challenging.

Thanks for being here. It is my sincere hope that the breathing tips you will discover on these pages will bring you happiness, health, balance, and radiance. Breathe!

~ Deborah Garland

BREATHE
in and out
again and again
...

Breath is precious. Treat it like a valuable, radiant gem. Take care of your breath. Pay attention to it. Shower it with love and care and respect and more love. Breath is your dearest friend..for life. ♡

Slow down your breathing. Close your eyes. Fill your lungs as slowly, deeply and evenly as you can. When you feel that your lungs are completely full, expand and bring in just a little bit more air. Slowly and gently and smoothly let your breath flow out. Feel your lungs deflate. Do it again and again. Keep your throat soft as you transition from inhale to exhale. Slow down some more until you feel ease and relaxation.

 # Breathe

Your first breath begins at birth, and your last breath at death. Fully celebrate and embrace the beautiful magnificence of each breath in between.

WHEN WE ORGANIZE OUR BREATH, WE ORGANIZE OUR LIFE.

~Dr. Vasant Lad

Focus your awareness into your breathing until you discover oneness of breath, mind, senses, and all facets of life.

Learn to equalize the in-breath and the out-breath. Try it. Make your inhale last the same length of time as your exhale. Find a steady beat, then breathe in and breathe out to the same steady rhythm. Start with an easy length, maybe 3 beats in and 3 beats out. Once the breath is very smooth and even, then increase to 4 counts in and 4 counts out. Keep a continuous flow of breath and make the breath very smooth. Once you are comfortable with that count, increase by one. Steady. Slow. Deep. Even.

Deep breathing has a heating effect.
Shallow breathing has a cooling effect.

Forceful breathing has a heating effect.
Relaxed breathing has a cooling effect.

Fast breathing has a heating effect.
Slow breathing has a cooling effect.

Breathe deeply. Shallow breathing means no endurance, no patience.

~Yogi Bhajan

Start an intimate,
eternal love affair
with your breath.

Inhale NINE counts
Hold ONE
Exhale NINE counts
Hold ONE

Repeat 10 times

Breathe big and deep and rich and full.

Breathe through your **mouth** for one minute like you're climbing a flight of stairs.

Pause and breathe normally.

Now breathe through your **nostrils** for one minute like you're climbing a flight of stairs.

Pause and breathe normally.

HOW WERE YOUR BREATHS DIFFERENT?

Breathe sweetly. Feel love
and tenderness and gentle
caresses inside of each
and every lovely breath...
...like angel kisses.

Breath is, therefore, a subtle mirror of underlying neural and mental activity. When we are happy it is rhythmic, deep and slow, and when we are unhappy or tense it is gasping, sighing, shallow, fast and uneven.

~ Dr. Swami Shankardev Saraswati

- INHALE DEEP.

- PUCKER LIPS & EXHALE LIKE YOU ARE BLOWING OUT A CANDLE.

- INHALE MORE SLOWLY AND EVEN DEEPER.

- NOW BLOW OUT A CANDLE ACROSS THE ROOM.

- INHALE REALLY SLOW AND REALLY DEEP.

- NOW BLOW OUT A CANDLE THAT'S FAR INTO THE DISTANCE.

- REST.

Use your breath and focused
attention to send vital prana
deep into your inner being.
Intimately experience an
unlimited source of
renewable energy.

Breath returns us home.

❈ Sit with your partner, back to back. Adjust your postures, and be comfortable. It's a good idea to sit up on a folded blanket or a pillow to elevate your hips. You may link elbows with one another or simply allow your arms to rest in your laps or sides.

❈ Begin to breathe slowly, feeling your back bodies press against one another. Communicate nonverbally as you increase the surface of your backs connecting with one another. Breathe together slowly. Soften into each other. Try not to push each other out of balance, but make every movement very subtle and in harmony with your partner.

❈ Breathe with each other for as long as you like, experiencing harmony and intimacy. This feels so nice, you won't want to stop!

BECOME A KEEN OBSERVER OF YOUR BREATH.

Allow breath to breathe you. Sit and wait. Do nothing. Be still and wait. Breath will breathe you. Be still. Wait. Do nothing. Breath will come into you. Breath will flow out of you. Succumb to the natural ebb and flow of breath, of universal prana, of life.

Make a habit of observing
how you are breathing.
Become a perpetual breath-watcher!

Lie down on your back with knees bent and soles of feet on the surface below. Slowly breathe in and feel where the back body is making contact with the surface below you. Make any adjustments to your hips and pelvis to reduce arching your lower back. Feel the skin on your back begin to soften. ✿

Breathe slowly, deeply and evenly. Softly inhale and feel more of your back body spread and press into the floor. Feel the entire surface of your back expand and become heavier. Perceive the skin on your back soften even more. Relax and exhale. Breathe in slowly and deeply and allow the entire back surface spread wider and feel heavier as it melts into the surface beneath you. Relax deeply and exhale. Continue as long as you like. ✿

You may also practice back breathing while sitting up against a firm surface. Sit up straight where you can feel the back surface of your body gently press against the back of a chair, or any firm surface such as a wall or headboard of your bed. You may place a small pillow or folded towel in the curve of the lower back so that you can feel the entire surface of your back press against a surface. ✿

As you slowly and deeply inhale, feel your body widen. Soften the skin of your back and feel the surface of your back body gently press and expand across the firm surface of the support behind you. Relax and feel the mid back press into the firm surface. Breathe deeply. Relax a bit more on the exhale and feel the lower back begin to press into the surface behind you. Feel the skin on the back, shoulders and neck soften and lengthen. ✿

Slowly repeat as many times as you like, relaxing and expanding the back body on the inhale, and slightly elongating the spine on the exhale. ✿

BREATHE HAPPY TODAY

Breathe very Deep and

E X P A N D

❋ ❋ ❋ ❋ ❋ ❋

Your Awareness.

Set aside at least 15 minutes around sunrise and again around sunset to sit quietly and breathe consciously. Sunrise and sunset are auspicious times in the natural cycle of daily life when we are aligned with the rhythms of nature. Try it for one month. ...But be prepared for immense blissfulness! ❋

$\mathcal{P}$ranayama is a technique through which the quantity of prana in the body is activated to a higher frequency.

~ Swami Niranjananda Saraswati

BREATHE SLOWLY

———— ◆ ◆ ◆ ————

You must consciously notice every ingoing and outgoing breath, like a watchman, observe the continuous rhythm of the two breaths.

~ Swami Satyananda Saraswati

 **Breathe** your ribs

V E R Y   W I D E

then **slowly**
let the air escape
through pursed lips.

Pranayama will revitalize and give you the necessary energy to manage your daily problems and overcome all obstacles on your journey through life. During moments of anxiety, insecurity, fear and passion, instead of fighting with your mind through the intellect, take the help of pranayama and stabilize yourself. Systematic practice of pranayama will also remove diseases of the eyes, nose and throat. It is the way to mental peace, physical health, revitalization and longevity.

~ Swami Satyananda Saraswati

Follow your breath into the stillness,
into the place where
everything dissolves.
Suspend yourself there.

As you inhale, silently say the mantra, "So."

Allow your inner attention to move upwards with Sooooo - from the base of your spine to the top of your head.

As you exhale, silently say the mantra, "Hum."

Allow your inner attention to move down with Hummmm - from the top of your head to the base of your spine.

Continue for 10 minutes or more.

Soooooooo Hummmmm
    Sooooooooo Hummmmm
        Soooooooo Hummmmm.

Breath is the doorway into the vast dimensions of the inner relams of the mind.

Be patient and very gentle with your breathing. Consistent awareness of your breath - day in and day out - with conscious attention will yield vast benefits in your physical, emotional and spiritual wellbeing. Truly. Slow, steady and consistent is the way to go. ♡ ♡ ♡

Breathe with awareness, calm and contentment. As often as you can, simply try your best to breathe with awareness, calm and contentment.
The more you do it, over time, breathing in this way will become second nature.
You will become
AWARE, CALM AND CONTENT.

Draw breath inward and downward.
Come away from the thinking thought-filled mind into the
place where you open into the universe within yourself.

~ Rama Jyoti Vernon

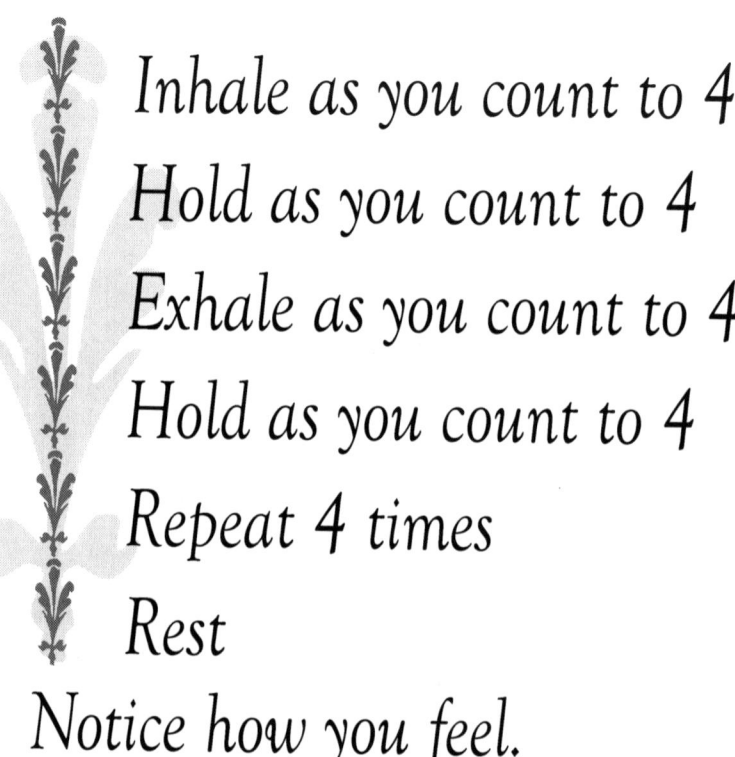

Inhale as you count to 4

Hold as you count to 4

Exhale as you count to 4

Hold as you count to 4

Repeat 4 times

Rest

Notice how you feel.

BREATHE DEEP AND
BROADEN YOUR BANDWIDTH

Whatever else is going on during the day, strive to continually redirect your awareness back to the breath. Then you will not lose your focus or become disturbed by anything.

~ Dr. David Frawley (Vamadeva)

Breathe in and out
of your
right nostril
to activate
your extrovert qualities.

I take refuge in the breath. Breath is all this, whatever there is, and all that ever will be. I take refuge in the breath.

~ Candogya Upanishad

Become very still and breathe smoothly, deeply and evenly. Begin to feel your entire body inflate as you breathe in. Feel your entire body relax as you exhale. Become aware of your entire body absorbing vital life force energy with every inhale. Feel your prana energize every cell in your body as you breathe out. Breathe in through your entire body. Feel vital prana permeate every atom. Exhale and feel your entire body release. Breathe in through your whole body. Breathe out through your whole body. Breathe in. Breathe out.

Your breath is a portal to instant infinity.

Set aside 10 minutes.
Get very quiet.
Listen to your breath.
Breathe slow, deep and even.
Heighten your senses.

Softly breathe smoothly, evenly and effortlessly. Observe your breath. Simply be aware of the movement of breath.

With your eyes closed, direct your attention to the tip of your nose. Be aware of the sensations of air present in the openings of the nostrils. Feel cool air flowing in, and warm air flowing out.

Feel your breath flow in through the nostrils, through the back of the throat, and down deep into the belly. Feel your breath softly flow out beyond your nostrils into the air beyond your body.

Breathe quietly, observing your breath for as long as you are comfortable.

Consistently breathe fully,
deeply,
evenly and
completely.
Breathe.

Soothe Your Nerves.

Gently close right nostril with your thumb.
Slowly breathe in and out through the
left nostril.

Calm Way Down.

INHALE JOY
EXHALE BLISS

BREATHE DEEP.
BROADEN YOUR BANDWIDTH.

inhale as you count to 4

exhale as you count to 2

inhale as you count to 6

exhale as you count to 2

inhale as you count to 8

exhale as you count to 2

inhale as you count to 10

exhale as you count to 2

then deeply rest.

FEEL YOUR BELLY BUTTON SOFTEN AND EXPAND
OUT AS YOU INHALE AND SMOOTHLY GLIDE BACK
IN AS YOU EXHALE.

Make your belly *big* and *billowy*
as you inhale.

Relax deeply as you exhale.
Blossom your diaphragm.

Take good care of the exhale - make it long and rich and fully complete.

The inhale will take care of itself.

Breathe quietly and direct your awareness to your nostrils. Feel air flow across the nasal rims, and inner and outer nostril linings. Notice how it feels as the air flows in. Notice how it feels as the air flows out. Softly flare the skin along the nostril openings. Feel the air there. Now stiffen the nostril openings. Feel the air.

Can you isolate the nasal openings and pulsate only the midsection of the nostrils? ✽

Make your inhale a thin stream of air.
Bring in a smooth, long, steady, slow breath.
Make it last as long as you can.

Pause and hold for a few seconds with no tension.
Blow out a steady stream of breath with pursed lips.

Rest.
Repeat 3X.

Throughout the day, become fully conscious of your breath. Observe how your breath fluctuates as you experience a diverse palette of thoughts, activities and emotions.

Practice pranayama
and you will know how to meditate.

~ Paramahansa Yogananda

Rhythmic, steady breathing helps you relax and integrate all of the body's systems and rhythms so they naturally work together in harmony.

Sit quietly and very, very still. Create a fine, thin thread of breath. Allow it to flow in and out almost imperceptively.

When you are short of wisdom, breathe.

~ Guru Nanak

Let the breath out to the very base of your being.

Relax around it.

Without using muscles, release more, and let it carry you deeper into the self.

Feel into the back body and back skull, intuitive side. Sink deeper into the subconscious, deep into the inner reaches of the self. Front of forehead rests to the back of head. Descend hairline skin to brows of the eyes.

Long, slow outbreath. Let go.

~Rama Jyoti Vernon

Broaden your perspective.

Breathe in and out very, very, very, very slowly and

see your awareness expand. ❋

Breathe naturally and become aware of feeling your body expand with the in-breath and deflate a little with the out-breath. Stay with this for a few moments.

Now as you breathe in, feel your body stretch tall. Feel elongation up and down. Feel as if the body is becoming very long and thin as the breath comes in. Relax as the breath flows out. Stay with this a few moments.

Now as you breathe in, feel your body stretch wide. Feel expansion out to the sides. Become very very wide as the breath comes in. Relax as the breath flows out.
Stay with this a few moments.

Now as you breathe in, feel your body expand outward in all directions - up, down and all around. Relax as you exhale. Radiate in all directions from your center, out into infinity as the breath fills you up. Relax as you exhale.
Stay with this for a few moments.

Then become very still and rest.

Breath is movement, and like movement, it is not something that we do, but who we are. If we learn to release all inhibitions around our breath, we learn to manage stress.

~Bhavani Maki

BREATHE THROUGH THE VERY
CENTER OF YOUR NOSTRILS IN
A STEADY THIN STREAM,
WITHOUT DISTURBING ANY TINY
HAIRS OF THE NASAL LININGS.

Be still
and very, very patient.

Be soft and quiet and still.

allow perfect waves
of pristine breath
flow deeply
through
you.

🌷 Sit up nice and tall either in an easy cross-legged position, or in a chair with the feet firmly placed on the ground. Take a few slow, deep and easy breaths. Relax the shoulders and face.

🌷 Place your left hand on your lower belly just under the navel and the right hand just above the navel. Take a big breath in and then expel all of the breath out.

🌷 Feel the belly draw back to the spine as the air leaves. Press your palms slightly against the abdomen as you breathe in. The belly will press against your palms. Feel the breath fill into the front, sides and back of the abdominal wall. Keep a gentle but firm pressure of your palms on the belly, and feel your abdomen expand a bit as presses into the palms. Feel the sides and back of the abdomen expand as breath comes in. The belly deflates back to the spine as you breathe out.

🌷 Repeat for several minutes. When you are ready to end the practice, lower your hands and take a few deep, full breaths. Begin to breathe spontaneously and naturally. Pause, rest and notice how you feel.

The mind becomes steady after Pranayama.

Breathe Deep.

Slow and Deep.

forget quick and shallow.

Dive in Deep.

Exhale all of your breath out.
Inhale slowly and deeply into the belly.
Retain your breath for a brief time as you imagine your body expanding in all directions, inflating as big as you can possibly imagine.
Exhale fully.
Rest and relax.
Repeat up to 5 times.

*Take a deep, full breath
and see where it goes.*
❧❧❧

When you master your breath, you
master your emotions.
When you master your emotions
you can master your mind.
When you master your mind you
can master your life!

- Mary Bruce

Without using your fingers to close your nostrils:

Breathe in through the right nostril very slowly.

Pause.

Slowly and smoothly breathe out through the left.

Inhale through the left, exhale right.
Then inhale right, exhale left.
Continue for as long as you like.

When you are ready to complete the practice, breathe naturally and observe a sense of balance and calm.

Let go of control.
Trust that the breath will fill you.

breath is real life

life is real breath

really breathe

really live!

Find your pulse.
Become quiet and still.
Listen until you find your heart's rhythm.
Count how many beats it takes you to inhale.
Exhale the same number of beats.
Keep this rhythm for 10 rounds.

☀ Follow the path of your breath. Feel your awareness go with the air into the nose, throat, heart, diaphragm, and deep down into the belly behind the navel, where you will experience a natural pause.

☀ Stay in this pause for a brief moment, and then follow the breath as you exhale. Go with your breath as it reverses its path up from the navel behind the diaphragm, heart, throat, through the nostrils, and out of the body to about nine inches in front of the nose to a second pause.

☀ The first pause is behind the belly button and the second pause is outside the body in space. At these two pauses, breath stops, time stops.

☀ Movement of breath is time. In these two pauses, feel that only pure existence is present, divinity is present. Allow yourself to feel suspended in space and time. When the breath stops, you become like an empty vessel. You merge effortlessly and silently into divinity.

☀ Continue slowly. Breathe slowly into your navel and suspend. Breathe out to a point beyond your nostrils and suspend. Release all thoughts and feel calm and peaceful.

Breathe into the heart of love, and cherish the beautiful power of deep intimacy that dwells within every breath.

The practice of pranayama will open you up to a greater view, and awareness of yourself... your inner self, your actions, your emotions, your patterns. Conscious breathing can lead you to discover wonderful, magnificent aspects of your true self that you were not yet aware of. Pranayama unlocks your own mega treasure chest that can't wait to pour out it's riches to enhance your life.

Pulsate and activate
your navel center.
Charge it up and feel
your inner
magnetism.

Inhale in 4 distinct strokes - like a sniff.
Exhale in 4 strokes.
Stay relaxed.
Keep a steady rhythm.
Make sure the breath stops at each stroke.
Activate your navel with each stroke.
Continue for one minute.
Then relax, breathe normally and rest.
Notice how you feel.

If you'd like to do one more round...
Try again and speed up the pace a bit.
Remember to use your belly button and
completely stop between strokes.

❀ BREATH REFLECTS YOUR STATE OF MIND ❀

Soften the bridge of your nose. Observe how your breath travels through the nostrils.

Is there friction? Can you soften the friction?

Quiet the waves of the mind. Friction of your breath can create too much conflict between the breath and the membranes of the nostrils.

Breathe in such a way that does not disturb a single hair in the nostrils. Breathe so there is no friction against the membranes of the nostrils.

Equalize breath between the right and left nostrils. How gently can you draw breath in? How effortlessly can you let it go?

PRANAYAMA
IS
MINDFULNESS

✿ Either seated or lying down, place your palms on the lower ribs.

✿ As you inhale, feel your ribs expand outward, pressing into your palms.

✿ You may apply gentle, light pressure against your ribs with your palms.

✿ Feel your ribs widen as your diaphragm strengthens and expands.

✿ Continue for several minutes then rest.

*Savor the slow, sweet rhythm of your breath
and marinate in the deep, still
silence of your soul.*

Sit up nice and tall.
Take a big, deep inhale.
As you exhale, chant "OM"
Make the sound last as long as your exhale.
"OOOOOOOOOOOOOOOOOOOOOOOmmmm"
Gradually lengthen your exhales.
Continue for 5 to 10 minutes or more.

When you are upset and feeling bad, take a long deep breath.

we share one breath, one love

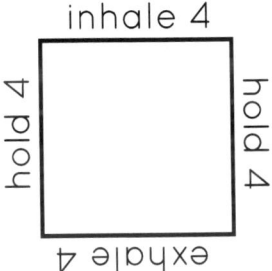

inhale 4

hold 4

hold 4

exhale 4

INFLATE as you inhale.
relax as you exhale.

Lie down with your knees bent so you feel your entire back supported. Make sure your lower back is not arched. Place one hand to your abdomen, and the other to your heart.

Bring your awareness to the places where your body meets the warmth of your palms. Imagine these places are portals of breath and deep awareness.

Slowly begin to breathe through your nose, inhaling and exhaling rich, slow, deep and even. Send your breath to where your hands are. Lengthen your exhale so that it is longer than your inhale.

Continue for as long as you like, Notice a sense of stability and calmness growing.

That is the best vitamin; that is the best
health capsule you can ever take—your own
breath of life.

~ Yogi Bhajan

Find thousands of sparkling bursts of energy vibrating throughout your breath. Feel every cell in your body pulsate with vibrant life force as your breath fills them with vital prana.

Invite breath in.
Let it stay awhile.
Enjoy its company.
Let your joy linger
long after the breath travels on.

Breath awareness alone can bring about
profound transformation -
physically, emotionally and spiritually.

Breath is calm when the body is calm.
The body is calm when the breath is calm.

Be delicate with this.
It takes only a flutter to shift the balance.

By controlling the breath we can influence the functions of our nervous and cardiovascular systems and the brain. We induce a state of relaxation.

"The source of the breath is the same as that of the mind. Therefore the subsistence of either leads to the other. The practice of stilling the mind through breath control is called yoga."

~ Sri Ramana Maharshi

breathe breathe breathe breathe breathe breathe
breathe breathe breathe breathe breathe breathe
breathe breathe breathe breathe breathe breathe
breathe breathe breathe breathe breathe breathe
breathe breathe breathe breathe breathe breathe
breathe breathe breathe breathe breathe breathe
breathe breathe breathe breathe breathe breathe
breathe breathe breathe breathe breathe breathe
breathe breathe breathe breathe breathe breathe
breathe breathe breathe breathe breathe breathe
breathe breathe breathe breathe breathe breathe
breathe breathe breathe breathe breathe breathe
breathe breathe breathe breathe breathe breathe
breathe breathe breathe breathe breathe breathe
breathe breathe breathe breathe breathe breathe
breathe breathe breathe breathe breathe breathe
breathe breathe breathe breathe breathe breathe
breathe breathe breathe breathe breathe breathe
breathe breathe breathe breathe breathe breathe
breathe breathe breathe breathe breathe breathe
breathe breathe breathe breathe breathe breathe

Emphasize deep breath and radiant heart all ways.

✻ Lie down and become aware of your whole body. Take several breaths simply being aware of your whole body. Observe. Feel. Simply lie still, breathe slowly and be keenly aware for a few minutes. Feel the weight of your entire body rest on the surface below you. Breathe into the shape of your body. Feel your whole body expand a little as the breath comes in. Feel your whole body deflate just a little as the breath goes out. Stay with this a few moments. Feel your whole body gently expand and yield as the breath flows in. Feel your whole body deflate just a little when the breath leaves.

✻ As breath slowly flows in, imagine your entire body inflating, expanding in all directions, like a balloon in the shape of your body. Begin to lengthen your exhale. As you exhale, keep the feeling of expansion but allow the body to deflate just a little as the breath flows out. With every inhale, feel the self-balloon grow larger and larger. Keep the sensation of expansion but deflate ever so slightly as you extend the exhalation. Expand and inflate with every inhale. Deflate ever so slightly as you slowly exhale. Continue to inflate yourself to the size of a voluminous balloon. Expand larger than the earth, the sun, our galaxy, the universe. Retain the expansive feelings as you prolong your exhale. Continue to breathe in this way for as long as you like.

Direct your attention to a part of your body.
Become still and quiet.
Focus intently on that part.
Keep focusing there and slowly breathe in.
Direct your breath into that part of your body.
Keep focusing there and slowly breathe out.
You are flooding that part of your body with vital life force energy.
Continue for as long as you like.

ENERGY FLOWS
WHERE AWARENESS GOES

As you go about your day, try to be aware of how you are breathing. At first, you will need to remind yourself to check in with your breath, but if you make it a habit, over time, awareness of breath will become a natural part of your day. You'll find yourself paying attention to your breathing while driving, at the supermarket, while cooking, at the office... everywhere! And that's a really good thing because being aware of your breath means you are fully present in the moment. Breath awareness is life awareness. It's beautiful!

Learn to breathe deeply and fully and observe all areas of your life bloom into the brilliant expression of your truest, most sublime self.

Sit or lie down comfortably.
Breathe slowly and evenly for a few
moments.

Count "ONE" to yourself as you exhale.
Next time you exhale, count "TWO."
On the next exhale, count "three," and so
on until you reach "five."

Once you reach "five," begin a new cycle,
silently counting the exhales.

♦   ♦   ♦   ♦   ♦

※ ※ ※ ※ ※ ※ ※ ※ ※ ※ ※ ※

Just as a drop of water merges into oneness with the ocean, surrender the breath from the lungs to become the one cosmic breath that breathes us all.

Breathe big, deep and full and feel your energy inflate every cell in your body

Keep the feeling of expanded, vibrant energy as you slowly and fully exhale

Feel prana, your vital life force energy travel through your body inside of your breath

BREATHE IN AS SLOWLY AS YOU CAN.
FILL YOUR LUNGS ALL THE WAY.
PAUSE BRIEFLY.

BREATHE OUT AS SLOWLY AS YOU CAN.
EMPTY YOUR LUNGS ALL THE WAY.
PAUSE BRIEFLY.

Breath and body are intertwined.
Breath and mind are intertwined.
Breath and emotions are intertwined.
Breath and infinity are intertwined.
Breathe. Breathe. Breathe.

❋ We can achieve tranquility simply by observing our breath. Amazing! ❋

Breath and the mind are intimately connected. As you breathe slowly, deeply and consciously, meditation will happen all on its own. Pranayama is the bridge between body and mind. Conscious breathing makes meditation accessible. As your mind becomes absorbed in awareness of breath, deep states of meditation can be achieved, effortlessly.

Love is the source of understanding.
Love is the source of breath. ♡
Breathe Unconditional Love.

♡♡♡

Become fully immersed into
the movements of
consciousness flowing
deeply within your breath.
Allow your breath to
completely absorb you.

Send your awareness down to the center of the navel. Soften the largest breathing muscles. Relax your diaphragm from the back, from the sides, from the front. Let go of the hardness and tension that lodge in the diaphragm. Release. Allow and relax.

Recieve a slow gentle breath then Let it go.

Soften all around the center of the navel. Allow it to release and let go. Release the tightness, and protectiveness and feel lightness in the navel.

Recieve a slow, deep, gentle breath...
then Let it go.

☙ Inhale through the right nostril for 2 counts.

☙ Hold 4.

☙ Exhale through the left nostril for 4 counts.

☙ Hold 2.

☙ Inhale through the left nostril for 2 counts.

☙ Hold 4.

☙ Exhale through the right nostril for 4 counts.

☙ Hold 2.

Repeat 5 times.

inhales seamlessly flow into exhales and
exhales seamlessly flow into inhales in smooth
unbroken waves

We can control our levels of nervous, muscular and emotional tension through breath control.

Lie comfortably on your back and wrap your arms around yourself. Feel your lower ribs with your palms and fingers. Relax your shoulders. Just hug yourself. Soften the skin on your face. Relax your chest. Feel your ribcage expand and relax. Feel your folded arms elevate and lower as your belly swells and deflates.

Breathe in love.

Breathe out love.

Inhale more love, Exhale more love.

Focusing complete and conscious attention on the flow of inhalation and exhalation, we travel deeper and deeper until we merge with the originating point of all of creation.

Sit up tall or lie down keeping a straight spine.

 Focus awareness at your root.
Inhale and bring breath from root to navel.
Exhale from navel to root.
Repeat 5 times.

 Focus awareness at your navel.
Inhale from navel to heart.
Exhale from heart to navel.
Repeat 5 times.

 Focus awareness at your heart.
Inhale from heart to third eye center.
Exhale from third eye to heart.
Repeat 5 times.

 Now inhale from your root to the top of your head
Exhale from the crown to the root.
Repeat 5 times.

Then breathe normally and notice how you feel.

Bring awareness to your nostrils.
Breathe slowly, feeling the air enter and exit the nostrils.
Bring each breath up to a point at the top - to the eyebrow center.
Make the breath very very slow and steady.
Breathe smoothly in this way for a little while.

Now guide your breath in along the inner part of the nostril linings.
Flow your breath out along the outer part of the nostril linings.
Breathe smoothly in this way for a little while.

SLOW, STEADY BREATHING WITH THE
So Hum MANTRA CAN HAVE A TREMENDOUS EFFECT
IN STABILIZING THE MIND AND EMOTIONS.

BREATHE

PAY ATTENTION

BREATHE

PAY ATTENTION

BREATHE

PAY ATTENTION

BREATHE

PAY ATTENTION

BREATHE

"To follow the way the spine functions during this process of breathing is of the greatest interest. The wave of expansion while exhaling, originating from the spine, is the basis of our teaching."

~ Vanda Scaravelli

Gradually smooth away any jerkiness or
irregularities, so that the breath is
silky and refined.

The roughness and choppiness in the breath
comes from the mind.

Calming the breath will calm the mind.

"Inhale and exhale systematically with close attention to the rhythmic pattern of breath, as a spider symmetrically weaves its web and moves to and fro along it."

~ B.K.S. Iyengar

✳ Lie down on your back, bend your knees and place the soles of your feet on the surface beneath you. Breathe slowly and relax.

✳ Become aware of the sacrum, the flat bony structure at the base of your spine. Slowly begin to move the hips, tracing the outline of the sacrum on the surface below you. Roll around the edges of the sacrum in one direction for a few moments, then reverse. Eventually, come to a still point and rest. Notice any feelings and sensations.

✳ Next begin to slowly inhale as you press the lower edge of the sacrum, nearest the tailbone, into the surface beneath you. The upper edge will lift. As you slowly exhale, rock the sacrum so that the top edge presses into the surface beneath you. Inhale as the tailbone side presses down, exhale as the top edge presses down. Feel your navel soften, widen and expand as you inhale. Feel your navel pull in, contracting toward the spine as you breathe out. Keep the movement and breath very slow and steady. Develop a very slow and relaxed rhythm.

✳ Continue for as long as you like. When you are complete with the practice, pull your knees up into your chest and give yourself a hug. Then stretch the legs out and reach the arms overhead. Relax and notice how you feel.

Want to reduce anxiety?
Simply make your exhale last
longer than your inhale!

Lie down on your back, bend your knees and place the soles of your feet on the floor. Let your sacrum feel heavy and secure. Relax your belly. Really let it go soft. ❣

Slowly breathe in through your nostrils as you imagine that your lower belly is a water balloon filling up with water. Relax the belly. It will softly expand as more liquid breath fills in. ❣

Keep your face, throat and shoulders soft and relaxed. Slowly deflate as you imagine the liquid breath pouring of your body. You may breathe out through your mouth if you like. As you exhale feel the entire surface of the front body gently melt down into the back. Keep exhaling until all of the liquid breath is gone. ❣

Slowly fill the lower abdomen again, maintaining a fluid, liquid, gel-like quality of the breath. The belly expands in all directions. Slowly deflate until all of the liquid breath oozes completely out. ❣

Continue for as long as you are comfortable. Then pause and notice how you feel. ❣

Breathe smoothly, quietly, and evenly...
with no pauses between breaths.

Breathe with the ❀ DIAPHRAGM ❀

IT'S THE LARGE SHEATH OF MUSCLE CONNECTED ALL THE WAY AROUND THE INSIDE OF THE LOWER RIB CAGE. SEE IF YOU CAN FEEL YOUR DIAPHRAGM MOVE AS YOU BREATHE. TRY TO KEEP YOUR UPPER CHEST AND SHOULDERS RELAXED, AND FEEL THE MOVEMENT OF YOUR DIAPHRAGM AS YOU BREATHE IN AND OUT.
DIAPHRAGM BREATHING IS REALLY GOOD FOR YOU!!!

Focus on your navel. Be still and quiet and send your awareness to your navel. As breath comes in, feel your belly expand and your lower ribs expand. Your diaphragm is widening. As breath flows out, feel your navel move back toward your spine. The center of your diaphragm is pulling up under your ribcage and your belly relaxes. Relax and breathe in this way very slowly and deeply. Your mind will become calm and you will feel balanced and tranquil.

Let breath move you.

Be soft, be calm, be still. Allow breath to come in.

Feel it. Embrace your breath.

How does your body want to move?

Where is breath taking your arms? Your legs?

Your shoulders? Your hips?

Let your magnificent breath guide your body.

Let breath move you.

Slightly widen the nostril tips as you inhale.
Refine your sensitivity around
the inner nostril openings.
Subtly entice your gentle breath to waft inward.

❀ ❀ ❀

Set a timer for one minute. Put your hands on your abdomen and inhale and exhale slowly, keeping track of the number of inhales you take.

The idea is to breathe fully and deeply...
the slower the better!

Smile, breathe and go slowly.

~Thích Nhất Hạnh

JUST BREATHE THROUGH IT.

"There is an intimate connection between the breath and nerve-currents. Control of breath leads to the control of vital inner currents"

~ Swami Sivananda Saraswati

How are you breathing right now?

Inhale big as you stretch your arms wide out to the sides. Open your palms and stretch your fingers wide. Keep inhaling as you stretch from the center of your heart all the way past your fingertips.

Exhale as you slowly bring your palms together at your heart with your thumbs lightly touching at the center of your heartspace.

Sit comfortably in a chair or floor cushion. Relax your shoulders and face, and make your spine straight and tall. Begin to breathe smoothly and deeply. Keep your shoulders wide, not rounded. In this practice, only the head moves. The shoulders, torso and legs stay still.

Exhale deeply. Inhale slowly as you smoothly and gently turn your head left. Pause. Exhale very slowly to the center. Pause.

Inhale very, very slowly as you turn head right, pulling up vital energy from the root. Pause. Exhale very slowly to center. Pause.

With your head at the center position, inhale very slowly as you gently lift your chin a little. Keep your sternum lifted, chest soft, shoulders relaxed. Pause. Release and exhale very slowly to center.

As you breathe in, feel your vital life force energy rising up from the base of the body. Your breath and subtle movement is pulling your prana up the spine, removing blockages and stagnation that collects in the lower centers.

Continue for as long as you like. Remember, it is a very gentle but profound practice. Go very, very slowly and breathe softly. You are elevating your prana to nourish the upper centers in your body.

Breathe and pull up vital prana shakti from
its sleepiness in your root.
Pull it up through all the vital centers.
Pull it up into the crown.
Radiate into infinity.

Practicing conscious breathing while walking is a great way to work pranayama into a busy day.

The easiest form of walking pranayama is timing your breath with your steps. Simply find a rhythm. There is no right or wrong way to do this.

Perhaps you take 5 steps per inhale and 5 steps per exhale.

Or walk very briskly, taking 10 steps per inhale and 10 steps per exhale.

Maybe you take 15 steps on the inhale then exhale all at once on the exhale.

Create your own rhythms... the possibilities are endless!

Consistency is the most important factor, especially if you want to gain the full benefits of pranayama. Practice every day. Make it a habit!

Breath is naturally infused with energy - with light.
Close your eyes and breathe into your inner body.
Expand your entire inner body with light-filled breath.
Keep breathing and expanding until you
observe your inner body flooded with light.
Your inner body will eventually appear fully
illuminated, just as if you turned on a
lightswitch to the inner spaces within you.

Breath exists on all planes and in all dimensions. Conscious breathing allows you to transcend the limitations of your thinking mind. ✿

BREATHE

Relax 🌼

BREATHE

Relax 🌼

BREATHE

Relax 🌼

BREATHE

Relax 🌼

A SLOW STEADY BREATH
IS HIGHLY BENEFICIAL.

A yogi measures the span of his life not by the number of years but by the number of breaths.

~ *Swami Sivananda Saraswati*

Be still. Breath arises out of stillness. Breath inflates, expands life, then returns to stillness in a never ending cycle.

Don't worry. Just take a big, deep breath. ♥♥

If your breath is very deep in the lungs,
it will give you a good red blood. Good red
blood, with the oxygen, is quite sufficiently
empowered to take away
impurities. When the lungs start clearing
the blood, then the liver, spleen, and kidneys
have much less work to do.

~ Yogi Bhajan

Breathe into your lower belly and ribs. Place your left hand on your lower belly just below your navel, and place your right hand on the outer right edge of your rib cage so you can feel your side ribs expand and relax.🌷

As you inhale feel your belly expand, then feel your ribs expand. As you exhale feel your ribs deflate, then your belly. Exhale completely as you press your palm very gently on your abdomen to help release your breath. Do this a few times until it begins to feel easy and natural.🌷

Now rest your right hand by your body and slide your left hand to your collarbone. As you slowly inhale, fill up the belly, then the mid chest and finally the upper chest. Feel your collarnes swell into your left palm as your chest broadens and rises.🌷

Fully exhale, first from the upper chest, mid chest. and abdomen, Your navel descends toward your spine.🌷

Relax and continue yogi breathing with both arms by your body. As you inhale, your belly lifts, then ribs expand, and the chest rises all the way up to the collarbones. As you exhale, collarbones release, your chest drops, ribs deflate, and your belly softens and lowers. 🌷

Continue for as long as you feel comfortable.🌷

Joyfully celebrate your breath. Celebrate each and every life-sustaining breath. Celebrate the highest breaths celebrate the lowest breaths, and rejoice in the infinite, blissful spaces between.

Observe your breath. What are you observing? What is the texture of your breath? How does is feel? What is the temperature? Does your breath feel spacious? Does it feel congested? What speed is it traveling? How deeply does it go into your body? How much effort does it take to inhale? How much effort does it take to exhale? How are you breathing right now? Can you describe how you are breathing right now?

Inhale as you count to 6
Exhale as you count to 6

Inhale as you count to 6
Exhale as you count to 6

(keep it going)

Inhale 6
Exhale 6

Inhale 6
Exhale 6

Inhale 6
Exhale 6

Inhale 6
Now Exhale as you count to 12

Rest.

"Let the breath be longer so that you can live longer, healthier and richer."

~ Yogi Bhajan

Observe the flow of breath through your nostrils. Which nostril is flowing more air?

When the left nostril is flowing, it's a good time to be more contemplative and introspective... a good time to meditate.

When the right nostril is flowing, it's a good time to be more active and extroverted... and a good time to eat!*

*... yogi weight management tip. When your right nostril is flowing, your metabolism is more efficient!

Slow down your breath.
Control your inale to make it very very slow.
Control your exhale to make it very very slow.

"If you do pranayama half an hour daily, you will never fall sick."

~ Swami Ramdev

Make your breath so pure and light that it feels as though you are not breathing at all.

170

Of all the body's automatic processes, the breath is the easiest to become aware of because it lies at the interface of the conscious and subconscious mind. We can easily take control of it whenever we want, though at most times it goes on by itself controlled only by the autonomic nervous system. It is, therefore, a subtle mirror of underlying neural and mental activity. When we are happy it is rhythmic, deep and slow, and when we are unhappy or tense it is gasping, sighing, shallow, fast and uneven.

~ Dr. Swami Shandardev Saraswati

Begin with a simple practice for inhalation, exhalation and holds.

 Try this progressive sequence:
>
> Inhale as you count to 4,
> Hold your breath **in** gently as you count to 4,
> *(Stay very relaxed in the throat and shoulders)*
> Exhale as you count to 8

 Stay with that rhythm for a good while. Practice a few times a day for a week or more. When your breath is even and smooth with no stopping or gripping, then progress to:

> Inhale as you count to 4,
> Hold your breath **in** gently as you count to 4,
> Exhale as you count to 8,
> Hold your breath **out** gently as you count to 4

 Notice how calm, balanced and happy you've become!

Bring your awareness UPWARD on the Inhale.

Bring your awareness DOWNWARD on the exhale.

"Because of the power of pranayama practice, one develops strength in the bones, the bone marrow and the heart; one develops the brain, the head, the anna kosam, the fat layer, the mana kosam, the strength of breath and prana, and longevity; it sharpens the senses, strengthens the intellect and the voice and purifies the blood. All these are important factors necessary for the maintenance of health."

~ Sri T. Krishnamacharya

❀ Breathe through the right nostril for heating and stimulating effects.

❀ Breathe through the left nostril for cooling and calming effects.

...breath is the meeting place of body, mind and spirit.

Every cell in your body breathes. Every cell pulsates and undulates with the organic rhythm of individual life force in synch with universal prana. Our breath flows in and out in natural rhythm, just as the ebb and flow of ocean waves onto the shore continually roll and fade to a comforting, life-sustaining pulse. Listen to your body breathe. Hear and feel the rhythm. Pulsate. Expand. Relax. Breathe.

Allow your breathing to become a meditation.
Practice conscious, mindful breathing.
In this way, your becomes a meditation.
Practice conscious, mindful living.

"... the practice of pranayama regulates that flow of prana throughout the body. It also regulates all the sadhaka's thoughts, desires and actions, gives poise and the tremendous will power needed to become a master of oneself."

~ B.K.S. Iyengar

The importance of breath cannot be overstated.

Flare your nostrils. Relax them. Flare. Relax. Flare. Relax. Now softly expand the entire surface of the inner nostril lining as you gently and slowly draw a smooth breath up the nasal passages. Pause. Softly allow your breath to float out.

Honor the sacredness of breath.

Inhale joy, peace, forgiveness and infinite happiness. Feel these uplifting qualities penetrate into you and infuse into you a sea of bliss. Exhale eternal love.

Breath is Limitless, Boundless, Infinite

Let go. Really let go. Allow breath to happen. Don't try to do anything about it. Simply get out of the way and consciously allow breath to happen to you - every bit of you.

Attune to your breath. Learn to dance with it. Allow the breath to lead. You are ac-customed to living life with the mind, the mind layer. But attune to your breath. Allow your breath to lead. Live. Live fully and be. Be fully present. Allow your breath layer to harmonize your body layers, your mind layers, and your high, fine, subtle layers – your highest layers
– where angels live.

Pranayama practice purifies our
body, mind and spirit -
cleansing, detoxifying, rejuvenating.

If you do absolutely nothing at all, you will continue to breathe. It's automatic. Breathing will happen naturally even when you are not paying attention to the breath. But you can also control how you breathe. You can consciously manipulate the pace, length, volume and rhythm of each breath to activate the immense power of life force energy within the breath - Prana. The more you pay attention to how you breathe, the better you will breathe. You will develop healthy breathing habits that help keep you calm and balanced through times of stressful situations in your life. Practice conscious, moment to moment breath awareness. ♡

Pranayama helps to
regulate one's conduct
and energy perfectly.

~ B.K.S. Iyengar

As you go through your day, breathe consciously
and intend to vibrate only the purest, clearest,
highest pranas.

BREATHE BIG TODAY

Breathe in and out rhythmically, rapidly and vigorously. Feel the immense power, energy and radiant vitality of your magnificent breath.

Powerful breathing can really boost your confidence! Try it. Next time you need to feel more sure of yourself, or feel that you need to exude extra radiance and positive energy, try a powerful breath. A good method is to breathe powerfully in and out in a steady rhythm while strongly sending your navel back to your spine on each exhale. Keep your pelvic floor lifted while you are breathing in and out in this way so you are sending your energy moving upward. Breathe like this for 30 seconds then rest. Do it again for one minute then rest. Maybe do it again for three minutes then rest. Feel your energy turbo boost! ☀

CONNECT your
❀
thoughts
❀
emotions
❀
body
❀
spirit
❀
and soul
❀
through BREATH.

〜

If something is really troubling you,
BREATHE THROUGH IT.
Sometimes situations in life become amplified
and you may not know how you are
going to make your way.
BREATHE IN ~ BREATHE OUT.
BREATHE with pure awareness.
BREATH carries wisdom to handle anything that
comes your way in life.
Your BREATH connects you with universal support
and divine, pristine,
unconditional love.
Now, and always.

BREATHE. BREATHE. BREATHE.

ॐ ॐ ॐ

By practicing pranayama correctly,
the mind is automatically conquered.

~ Swami Satyananda Saraswati

ॐ ॐ ॐ

Breathe fire...
combustion,
the powerful primal force of creation.
Ignite your soul.

Lots of us have a habit of taking shallow breaths, and not filling up the lungs fully. When you breathe in, try to expand the lungs and the belly. When you breathe out, completely relax your belly and release every bit of air from your lungs.

With slow, calm, deep and steady breathing, the mind obtains a state where separation merges into oneness.

Therefore pranayama should be done daily with a sattvic state of mind so that the impurities are driven out of sushumna nadi and purification occurs.

~ Hatha Yoga Pradipika II:VI

One day while practicing pranayama, you will realize that you have eased into a deep state of meditation. Your breath will be smooth and easy and your mind will be peaceful and clear. It will happen easily and effortlessly.

Feel your thoughts, speech and actions joyfully dance to the delightful rhythm of your breath!

Allow the breath to guide you. For a few moments, right now, allow your breath to inform you. You don't need to know what to do. Be still and quiet and gentle. Allow breath to breathe you. Go into the breath - deeply in. Feel. Listen. Be. Impulses of the most subtle nature will percolate through you and then you will know what to do.

inhale.
exhale.
rinse & repeat.

Sit or lie down and get comfy.

Place your fingertips softly on your navel.
Let your middle fingers lightly touch.

Breathe in fully and feel your belly inflate.
Your fingers will separate.

Breathe out and feel your belly deflate.
Your fingers will touch again.

～ Continue to breathe, soothe and relax ～

Some traditions measure the span of life not by the number of **years** between birth and death, but by the number of **breaths** between birth and death.
Breathe slowly.
Live fully.

Be patient.
Breathe.
Breathe patience.
Stay calm and patient.
Breathe.
Breathe.
Breathe.
Everything will be all right.

Would you like to experience increased energy, lightness, vitality, stamina, radiance, clarity of mind, and optimal brain performance? That's easy to achieve... simply practice pranayama!
It's good for you.

"From practicing only pranayama, it is possible to achieve long life and good health."

~ Sri T. Krishnamacharya

How **LONG** AND **WIDE** CAN YOU STRETCH YOUR BREATH?

❀ Radiate! Breathe and imagine your body as a big, beautiful starfish moving the breath from the belly button outward to the fingers and toes and beyond. Then allow the breath to come right back in, deep into the center of the navel.. Stand with your legs wide and arms outstretched. Find your navel undulating in and out as the breath ebbs and flows. Send breath radiating outward from the navel through the arms and legs. Feel breath travel along this path back into the navel.

❀ **S**it comfortably on a chair or cushion on the floor.

❀ **B**ring air in through both nostrils, as slowly and gently as you can.

❀ **R**etain the breath easily, softly and comfortably as you silently repeat 'OM' or other mantra.

❀ **E**xhale slowly and comfortably.

❀ **C**ontinue for 10 minutes, allowing the breath to remain deep, smooth, slow, relaxed and full.

"Whenever your breath becomes
shallow, you are irritated, irritable."
~ Yogi Bhajan

Savor the slow, sweet rhythm of your breath and
marinate in the deep, still silence of your soul.

Try synchronizing your inhale and exhale as you open and close your palms. Breathe in as you slowly spread the fingers wide. Bring as much breath in as you can and really stretch the hands... spread out the palms and webbing between fingers. Then as you very slowly exhale, relax the hands. Repeat and repeat. You might also feel like doing the same thing with your feet. Notice how by simply synchronizing your breath with easy movement helps you feel balanced, stable, calm, refreshed, and really happy! ❀

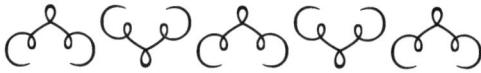

Profound insights and greater self-awareness can occur through the simple process of shifting attention from one nostril to the other.

The right nostril is associated with action, concentration, alertness, heat. Be aware of your breath flowing through the right nostril.

The left nostril is associated with sensitivity, introspection, calmness, coolness. Be aware of your breath flowing through the left nostril.

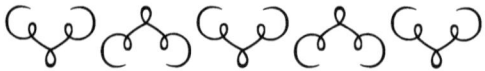

Breathe.

Breath connects energy and matter.

Breathe.

Breath connects consciousness and mind.

Breathe.

Breathe.

Just Breathe.

Rapidly, powerfully and fully inhale and exhale
8 times.
make the breath really big.

Then slowly and smoothly exhale and inhale
8 times.
expand and deflate the lungs.

First rapidly then slowly.
Repeat 8 times!

*B*reathe deeply into the center of
your spine.

Can you feel prana travel up the spine
as you inhale?

Can you feel prana flow down the spine
as you exhale?

Feel your spine get wider, taller
as breath comes in.

Feel your spine relax as breath flows out.

How are you breathing today?

Focusing on the act of breathing clears the mind of all daily distractions and clears our energy - enabling us to better connect with the Spirit within.

Listen to the sweetness of your precious breath and infuse divine nectar into each and every thought and each and every word.

♡ ♡ ♡ ♡ ♡ ♡ ♡ ♡

🌹 Are you still breathing in a
shallow manner, up high in the chest?
Is your breath kind of short and choppy?
TRY STRAW BREATHING!
It will slow down your breath and encourage
you to breathe fully and deeply.
IT'S EASY.
Hold a straw in your lips.
Inhale through your nose and
slowly exhale through the straw.
Don't blow out through the straw, just exhale.
Your out-breath will become longer and your
diaphragm will do it's job more efficiently.
🌹

❧ Divide your exhale into three parts. Try it.
Slowly inhale, then :

> Exhale a little - pause,
> Exhale a little more - pause,
> Exhale all the way.

Again, slowly inhale, then:

> Exhale a little - pause,
> Exhale a little more - pause,
> Exhale all the way.

Continue smoothly and easily.
If you are comfortable and at ease, maybe you'd like to try a four part exhale:
Slowly inhale, then:

> Exhale a little - pause,
> Exhale a little more - pause,
> Exhale a little more - pause,
> Exhale all the way.

Continue and notice your sense of calm, and balance. Finish by breathing slowly and normally.

Your exhale will become someone's inhale. Infuse it with love. Your inhale was once someone's exhale. Breathe love. Be love.

Simply keep coming back to your breath.

There is one way of breathing that is shameful and constricted. Then, there is another way: a breath of love that takes you all the way to infinity.

~Rumi

Words of yogi wisdom:

Breathe slowly...
Cherish your breath.
Cherish it and love it.
Cherish life.

Prana is not the breath. Prana is shakti, energy - subtle energy, life force energy. Prana is transmitted through our bodies and minds through our breath.

Pranayama is like a door or a gateway or a portal.
Through pranayama you enter the land of meditation.

Pranayama extends the dimensions
of prana - our vital life force energy.

PRACTICE CONSCIOUS BREATHING.
EVERY DAY. WITHOUT EXCEPTION.

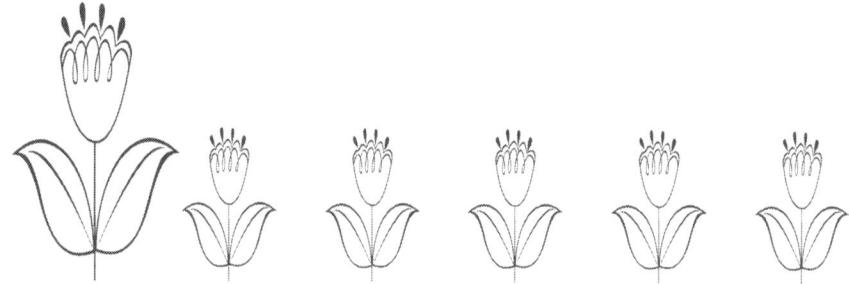

♡ Conscious breathing unites us with the vital currents of life which flow into and come out of our hearts.

Make your EXHALE last twice as long as your INHALE. Try to do this as often as you can... while in the supermarket line, waiting on a call on hold, or while just hanging out. Do it and you will be surprised at how relaxed and tranquil you become! ☀

Pranayama involves dimensions of space, time and beyond. Approach pranayama practice as an explorer of the vast and infinite.

● · · · ○ · · · ●

Let go of stress. Soothe your nerves and repeat a mantra as you breathe. Consciously breathe in the sound "Let" and consciously breathe out the sound "Go."

Inhale LET ~ Exhale GO

LET GO

LET GO

LET GO

Place one hand on your chest.
Place the other hand on your belly button.
Relax.
Breathe deeply for a few moments.
Feel your belly inflate and deflate.
Keep your chest still.
Breathe into the belly button hand.
Keep your chest hand quiet and still.
Breathe love into yourself through your belly button hand.
Breathe love into yourself through your chest hand.

Feel breath at the gentle openings of the nostrils. Feel breath slowly rise up through the cone-shaped nostrils up to a divine point of light at the center of the eyebrows. Linger there. Softly flow the breath downward and outward through the nostril cones and out the openings. Feel the point of light at the eyebrow intensify with a magnetic charge. Feel breath flow in through the nostril cones, attracted by centerpoint of light. Linger there. Release the breath from the point of light, out the nostrils and into space beyond.

"The yogi who shuts out the external sense-objects and fixes his concentration between the eyebrows, stabilizing the inward and outward breaths that flow through the nostrils and thus controls the senses, the mind and intelligence, is dedicated to the attainment of liberation. He is never bound by desires stemming from lust, fear and anger and is certainly always liberated."

~Bhagavad Gita - Chapter 5 - Verse 27-28

Breathe in perfect rhythm with someone you love. Try it!

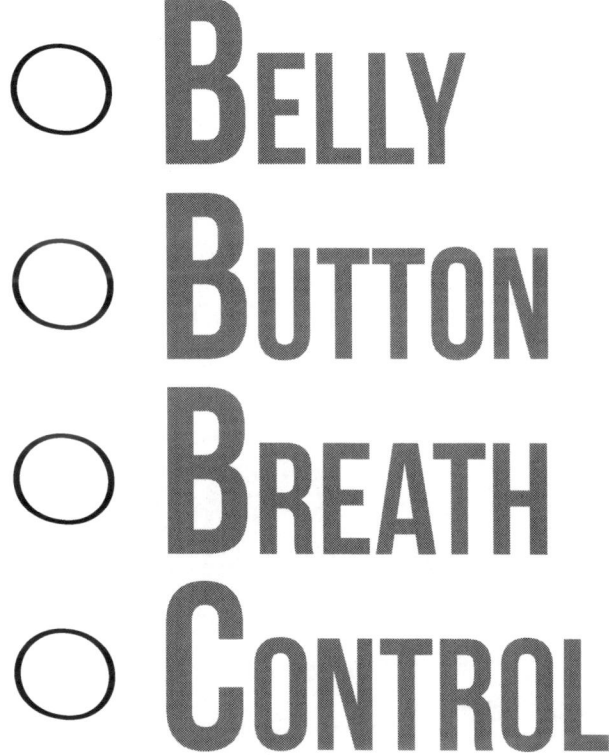

○ **B**ELLY

○ **B**UTTON

○ **B**REATH

○ **C**ONTROL

Open your heart wide so the universe can fill you with its breath.

Breathe in and out
through every pore
of your skin.

Pranayama allows you to move between a fast rhythm and a slow rhythm and to keep the brain under conscious control, to use the switches in the brain. You can speed your mind up if you want to. You can slow your mind down if you want to. You can slow your breath. Your breath is linked directly to the centre of your brain. As you breathe slowly in ujjayi or brahmari your brain waves become calm.

~Dr. Swami Shankardev Saraswati

Quick, shallow breathing will cause you to show premature signs of ageing.

So breathe slowly, deeply and fully to retain a youthful appearance. Beautiful!

Breath is perfection.
You are perfection.

Breathe

Breathe

Breathe

...Even if that's all you can do today.

Breathe

Breathe

Just Breathe.

❦❦❦

Breathe in pure light.
Illuminate every atom in your body.
Feel prana expand exponentially.
Radiate joyous luminosity.

❦❦❦

Breath is the bridge which connects life to consciousness, which unites your body to your thoughts.

~Thích Nhất Hạnh

- Gently close your right nostril with your right thumb.

- Inhale slowly through your left nostril.

- Release the right nostril and close the left nostril with your right ring finger.

- Exhale slowly through your right nostril

- Inhale slowly through your right nostril.

- Release the left nostril and close the right.

- Exhale slowly through your left nostril.

- Inhale slowly through your left nostril.

- Release the right nostril and close the left nostril with your right ring finger.

- Exhale slowly through your right nostril

- Inhale slowly through your right nostril.

- Continue for as long as you like, then rest. -

BREATHE IN DEEP.
HOLD FOR A BRIEF WHILE
BREATHE OUT SLOWLY.
HOLD FOR A BRIEF WHILE

What do you need from your breath at this moment?

Melt into your breath,
   melt into your soul,
      melt into infinity.

*Thoughts affect your breathing,
and breathing affects your thoughts.*

Set a timer for one minute. Breathe powerfully and deeply in and out for one minute...Try to keep your breath rate 15 or fewer rounds per minute.

(a round is one inhale and one exhale)

Breathe fully and deeply each time. Then rest.

Notice your energy boost! ♡

Breathe. Let go. And remind yourself that this very moment is the only one you know you have for sure.

~ Oprah Winfrey

Take several full, relaxed and slow breaths.

Then exhale all of your breath out quickly with vigor, powerfully popping your navel back to the spine. Then immediately relax and soften the belly and allow breath to naturally flow in.

Active, powerful exhale. Passive inhale.

Again exhale strongly while contracting the abdominal muscles, then relax the belly as the air flows back in.

The exhale is strong and powerful and the inhale happens effortlessly, naturally and passively.

Find a steady rhythm and practice 10 rounds.

Then pause, rest and breathe normally.

Nurture your ability to maintain continuous awareness of your breath as you go about your daily activities. Simply observe and feel the breath flow in and out... all day long!

Sometimes it's not so easy to:

Follow your breath.

Listen to your breath.

Hear only the sound of your breath.

Observe the flow of your breath.

Be patient. Be gentle with yourself. The mind can be bossy and try to take control. The mind likes to have a job to do. A perfect job for the mind is paying attention to something, one thing. Give your mind the job of focusing on one thing – your breath. When the mind gets bored and wants to move on to something else, remind the mind to stay with the job of focusing on the breath. Maybe you will have to remind your mind over and over and over again. That's ok, it's part of the process. Stay with it. Pretty soon you will not have to remind your mind to focus so much. Your mind will become steady, focused and calm.

Breathe consciously… and stay with it.

As you richly inhale, sense that you are receiving energy from a pure, eternal source of perfect divinity.

Feel every cell and atom in your body swell with abundant, fresh, pure, vital prana as you breathe in.

As you gently and slowly exhale, send your breath out very, very far. Send it far and deep into the limitless, infinite cosmos.

BREATHE

Slowly breathe deeply and evenly, and prepare to fully relax. Close your eyes, keep your lips together and teeth slightly parted.

Very softly close the flaps of your ears ever so lightly with your thumbs.

While gently exhaling, make a soft humming sound and feel the vibration of the humming inside your head. Hum for the entire duration of the exhale.

Continue to inhale gently and hum softly as you slowly exhale. Practice for several moments.

Keep your eyes closed, lower your hands and sit in silence. Observe how you feel.

Pranayama dissolves all that veils your inner light.

Rest your hands lightly on your belly button
and breathe there. Feel your belly expand and
relax under your palms. Your breathing will
become full and slow and deep.
It's very good for you.

Quick, shallow breathing is inefficient and not so good for emotional stability and balance. It's good to learn to slow down the breath and breathe deeply. Relax your body and pay attention to how you are breathing. Feel the breath. You can stop thinking about so many things... just focus on your breath and slow it down.

The next time you begin to feel angry, try to have the presence of mind to breathe slowly and very deeply. The waves of anger will soften to gentle ripples and eventually give way to peace and calm.

Breathe sweetly. Divine essence flows through your breath. Allow its sweetness in. Don't try, just allow. Breathe sweetly and softly. Feel your face soften. Observe your transformation as tension fades into peace. Breathe ever so sweetly, ever so tenderly. Breath is precious and so are you.

Shimmering, silvery, liquid moonlight.
Breathe. Luna, chandra, left channel of
the nostril. Breathe. Exhale cool prana
through Ida nadi, the left nostril. Drink
in divine, cool breath through Ida, the
feminine channel. Dissolve into her.
Dissolve into breath.

Need to chill down? Try this cooling, soothing breath called Sitkari.

❀ Curl the edges of your tongue until it makes a tube shape.

❀ Purse your lips and draw air in as if you were breathing through a straw.

❀ Close your lips and slowly exhale through your nose.

❀ Repeat for as long as you like.

Become very still and listen deeply to your breath. Breathe and listen. Breathe and listen. Listen closely. When you breathe softly enouth and listen closely enough, your deepest truths can be heard.

Breathe so softly that you can hear the
flutter of delicate
angel wings dancing on air.

Breath purifies your body,
your mind,
your emotions, your spirit.

Love your breath.
Pay attention to your breath.
Nurture your breath.
Treat your breath with tender loving care.
Your breath carries your life force.
It's always there for you.
It's your constant companion for life.

Inhale and spread your arms wide
Bring in as much air as you can into your lungs

Exhale all the breath out as you wrap your arms
around your body - giving yourself a sweet big bear hug

Breathe in only joy, light
and happiness.

Astound yourself with the
pleasure of simply breathing.

STICK OUT YOUR TONGUE AND BREATHE IN AND OUT - PANTING LIKE A DOG.

FEEL YOUR BELLY BUTTON POP BACK TO YOUR SPINE WITH EACH EXHALE.

KEEP A STEADY, RAPID RHYTHM.

CLOSE YOUR MOUTH AND CONTINUE THIS BREATH THROUGH THE NOSTRILS.

YOU'RE DOING BREATH OF FIRE.

STOP AFTER 1 MINUTE.

TAKE IN A SLOW, DEEP BREATH.

SLOWLY EXHALE.

REST.

REPEAT.

BREathe
Love

If something is weighing heavily on your mind and you feel troubled, give your thoughts a rest and breathe. Just breathe. Focus on breathing. No thinking, just breathing. Breathe in, breathe out. Just breathe.

Having repressed his breath in the body, and having checked his movements, one should breathe through the nostrils with diminished breath. Like that chariot yoked with vicious horses, the wise man should undistractedly restrain his mind.

~ Shvetashvatara Upanishad (II,9)

Learn to control your breathing
by interrupting the breath mid-stream.

Find a steady steady t rhythm - a steady beat.
Once you find your beat, then:
Inhale a little for 2 beats and stop.
Inhale a little more for 2 more beats then stop.
Inhale a little more for 2 more beats and stop.
Continue until your lungs are completely full.
-Make sure you keep your neck and shoulders relaxed the whole time-
Then exhale all the air out slowly and evenly.
Repeat a few times then relax completely.

INHALE. HOLD. EXHALE.

Pranayama has three movements:
prolonged and fine inhalation, exhalation
and retention; all regulated with precision
according to duration and place.

~ Yoga Sutras of Patanjali 2:50

Allow your breath to flow gracefully.

Sit up nice and tall.
     or lie down and keep your spine straight.

Inhale a little and feel your lower belly begin to inflate.

Inhale a little more and feel your chest and back expand.
          stay relaxed.

Inhale a bit more and feel your collar bones widen.
               keep your shoulders down.

Exhale a little and relax your collar bones and shoulders.

Exhale a little more and relax your chest and back.

Exhale all the way and pull your belly button to the spine.

Repeat. Repeat. Repeat.

breathe quietly.
listen to your breath.
do nothing but listen to the breath.
can you hear the secret sound that
vibrates deep inside the breath?
listen closely...

Sooooooooo Hummmmmmm

"When sound, breath, and awareness come together, it becomes light... So Hum meditation properly practiced leads to the union of the individual with the universal Cosmic Consciousness. You will go beyond thought, beyond time and space, beyond cause and effect. Limitations will vanish."

~ Dr. Vasant Lad

breathing

dreams

like

air.
- f. scott fitzgerald

Begin.
Begin this very moment.
Breathe.
Breathe In.
Breathe Out.
Begin Again.

*Inhale, and divinity
approaches you.
Hold the inhalation, and
divinity remains with you.
Exhale, and you
approach the divine.
Hold the exhalation, and
merge into divinity.*

STEADY YOUR BREATH. STEADY YOUR MIND.

With each and every breath cycle, fully empty every ounce of breath from your lungs.

Relax.

Soften to receive a flowing wave of brand new breath.- a sparkling infusion of fresh life force energy.

Awaken into a brand new beginning.

Sit up nice and tall.
Keep your spine straight.
Relax your shoulders.

Inhale slowly as you turn your head left.
move just your head... body stays still

Exhale slowly as you turn your head right.
keep your spine nice and straight

Continue with your eyes closed and focus
awareness at your eyebrow center.

sit or lie very very still.

observe your breathing.

do absolutely nothing at all but watch your breath.

observe your breath.

observe your breath.

observe your breath.

observe your breath.

observe your breath.

observe your breath.

observe your breath.

observe your breath.

observe your breath.

breathe in.
breathe out.
no thinking.
breathe in.
breathe out.
just breathe.
breathe in.
breathe out.
only love.
breathe in.
breathe out.
feel.
breathe in.
breathe out.
pure peace.
breathe in.
breathe out.
this is life.

∞ Bring in a slow, deep breath through your nose as you relax your shoulders and expand your lungs as much as you can – especially at the very top.

Stay relaxed and pause.

Softly purse your lips so they form a round "o" shape without puffing out the cheeks.

Quickly exhale every ounce of your breath out through the lips like a cannon blast.

Repeat 3 times. ∞

Explore the vast and infinite dimensions of your breath.

Counting your breaths can help you relax. Take in a really deep breath and feel the belly inflate larger and larger. Imagine that you are breathing through the belly button. Feel your belly expand and deflate with each inhalation and exhalation.

Now begin to concentrate and count each breath. Start from 100 and count back to 1. If you lose count, start again from 100. You will really need to pay attention and count and breathe. It will help you relax if you can count each breath from 100 back to 1 withoud making any mistakes, and also be aware of the belly inflating and deflating with each breath.

After you count from 100 back to 1 while breathing from your belly, then do the same thing only this time focus on your throat pit. Feel your breath in your throat and hear a gentle, soothing sound in your throat as you breathe in and out. Count your breaths from 100 to 1 while focusing on your throat.

If you would like to continue, next do the same thing while focusing on the nostrils. You will feel the breath become more subtle. Breathe softly while counting from 100 back to 1 while focusing on the nostrils. By now you should feel peaceful, tranquil and so relaxed.

There is a diamond filled with radiant light deep within the center of your heart. Focus your awareness there. Direct your breathing there. The moment you make contact, your entire being will illuminate with divine love. Unpleasant areas of the mind transform into bliss. Close your eyes and breathe deeply into the diamond of light within the lotus of your heart.

BREATHE

BREATHE

BREATHE

BREATHE

BREATHE

BREATHE

BREATHE

BREATHE

BREATHE

BREATHE

♡

Relax your belly and breathe the way a sweet little baby breathes.

♡

Most of us breathe incorrectly. We habitually use only a small part of our lung capacity. We breathe in a shallow manner, keeping us stuck in stress.

It's easy to breathe deeply. Just make it a habit. Practice deep breathing every day. Stress may not disappear altogether, but you will have a valuable tool for getting you through stressful times. ❀

❀ Inhale through the nose in seven parts, pausing at each chakra center - pelvic floor, pubic bone, navel, heart, throat pit, eyebrow center and suspending the breath at the crown.

❀ Exhale through the nose and imagine the breath as a fountain flowing up from the crown of the head and cascading down all around you, enveloping you with vital prana. Draw the breath in from the root and repeat.

❀ Practice this breath meditation for as long as you like. When you are ready to complete the practice, take in a big, deep breath and hold for a brief while.

❀ Breathe naturally and effortlessly and observe how you feel. Relax and rest.

MASTER YOUR BREATH.

Dive deeply into the very center of your breath.

Sitting in the padmâsana posture the yogî should fill in the air through the left nostril (closing the right one); and, keeping it confined according to one's ability, it should be expelled slowly through the sûrya (right nostril). Then, drawing in the air through the sûrya (right nostril) slowly, the belly should be filled, and after performing kumbhaka as before, it should be expelled slowly through the chandra (left nostril).

~Hatha Yoga Pradipika 2:7-8

Breathe in fully and deeply through your nose.

Open your mouth, widen and stick out your tongue so much that the tip wants to reach all the way to your chin.

As you exhale, pull your eyeballs up and in toward the center of your eyebrows and exhale powerfully making a deep "haaaaaaa" sound.

Close your mouth, soften the eyes and inhale from your nose.

Exhale again powerfully, sticking out the tongue and making it wide, with a deep "haaaaaaaa."

Practice a few times.
Then close your eyes and rest.

Breathe deeply.

Don't worry.

Breathe deeply.

Be light.

Breathe deeply.

Be happy.

BREATHE **BIG** TODAY ♡

Breath controls prana. This practice is called pranayama. It is the control of prana, the regulation of prana, or the withdrawal of prana from the external world back to its primal source. That is why pranayama is so important to practice systematically, regularly, day after day, so we get all the prana into a rhythm.

In this way we get a rhythm of the pure life force flowing through ida, pingala and sushumna and out through the aura. We gain a rhythm of awareness soaring inward, into refined states of the ajna chakra and sahasrara chakra, the perspective areas from which we are looking out at life as if we were the center of the universe. This is how we feel when we are in these chakras.

Pranayama will revitalize and give you the necessary energy to manage your daily problems and overcome all obstacles on your journey through life. During moments of anxiety, insecurity, fear and passion, instead of fighting with your mind through the intellect, take the help of pranayama and stabilize yourself. Systematic practice of pranayama will also remove diseases of the eyes, nose and throat. It is the way to mental peace, physical health, revitalization and longevity.

~ Kauai Hindu Monastery

*Breath is the cord
that ties the soul
to the body.*

Breath carries prana,
the life force we are born with.

This life force is a part of the
universal prana.

We can learn to breathe to
expand our prana.

We can learn to breathe to
expand our existence.

Become aware that your
inhalation expands from
within the deepest core of
your being towards your
highest consciousness.

Become aware that you
merge with your highest
consciousness as you exhale.

AS BREATH FLOWS DOWN INTO YOUR LUNGS, FEEL
YOUR PRANA - YOUR VITAL LIFE FORCE ENERGY -
RISE UP AND EXPAND THROUGHOUT YOUR BODY.

AS BREATH FLOWS UP AND OUT OF YOUR LUNGS, FEEL
YOUR PRANA - YOUR VITAL LIFE FORCE ENERGY -
DESCEND DEEP DOWN TO THE PELVIS.

Find a steady beat.
Inhale full and deep.
Exhale a little as you count 2 beats then pause.
Exhale a little for 2 more beats then pause.
Exhale a little for 2 more beats then pause.
Continue until lungs are completely empty.
Do it all again if you are comfortable.

Then breathe normally and relax. 🫶

Infinity
is found in this one magnificent breath.
Now,
in this one absolutely perfect moment.
Breathe.

*What would your life be like
if you made every breath
a breath of love?*

Separate the teeth ever so slightly, widen the sides of the mouth ,and place the tip the tongue just behind front teeth and touching the upper palate.

Sip in the air so it swirls in along the sides of the teeth and inner cheek lining, making a hissing sound. It will feel cool and refreshing.

Then close the lips, relax the tongue and exhale through the nose.

Continue for several minutes then rest. ❁

Just as a drop of water
merges
into oneness
with the ocean,
surrender
your breath from the lungs
to become
the one cosmic breath
that breathes us all.

INHALE THROUGH THE NOSE AS YOU COUNT TO 4

HOLD BREATH IN AS YOU COUNT TO 7

EXHALE STRONGLY THROUGH PURSED LIPS 8 COUNTS

REPEAT 4 CYCLES

INHALE 5, HOLD 5, EXHALE 5

INHALE 6, HOLD 6, EXHALE 6

INHALE 7, HOLD 7, EXHALE 7

INHALE 8, HOLD 8, EXHALE 8

INHALE 9, HOLD 9, EXHALE 9

INHALE 10, HOLD 10, EXHALE 10

Special breathing exercises unfold cellular intelligence and make the individual happy, peaceful and blissful.

~Dr. Vasant Lad

Be gentle with your nostrils.
They are portals of pure prana.

Getting a handle on your breathing can work wonders in your life!
Breath can help you feel calm, happy, refreshed and healthy! And it's totally free! You don't need any equipment and you can breathe anywhere, anytime! Yay! ♡

KEEP CALM

AND

BREATHE

Sometimes the mind can get very bossy.
Sometimes emotions can seem so big and get in the way of seeing clearly.
Sometimes thoughts spin round and round and loop over and over and over again.
But...
Breath can take care of all of that.
Breath will tame the mind.
Breath will put emotion into perspective.
Breath will clarify thoughts.
Breath purifies, balances, regulates, calms.
Breathe in.
Breathe out.
Breathe in.
Breathe out.

Slightly expand the nostril tips as you inhale.

Develop sensitivity around the
inner nostril openings.

Subtly entice your breath to gently waft inward.

When you send your breath out... it has no end. It travels beyond the boundaries of our solar system, our galaxy, our universe and through the mulitverses, merging into infinity.

As you allow a breath to travel in, the entire cosmos is breathing you.

BREATHE. PEACE.

"Whenever you are not sure what to do, bring your attention back to your breathing. The breath will take you into the feeling of the pose and then the inner feeling will start telling you what to do."

~ Erich Schiffman

Breathe in tenderly, gently, easily.
Receive the soft, gentle, loving
inner caress of your sweet, sweet breath.
Softly float your precious breath outward
to merge into the vast space beyond.
Soothe your soul.

Regular, consistent practice of rhythmic, conscious breathing creates a clear, sharp and intelligent mind.

Pranayama is designed to calm the nervous system, to allow the nerves to find a rhythm. A fast rhythm is necessary if you want to think or to cross the street, but a slow rhythm is necessary when you have reached your destination and want to relax.

Pranayama allows you to develop a broad range of experience. Relaxation is only one half. Sometimes you must be tense, you must be alert, but that tension must be in balance with your need, with your relationship with yourself and with your environment.

~ Dr. Swami Shankardev Saraswati

When you BREATHE
consciously you
instantly feel more vibrant,
radiant, youthful
and healthy.

Breathing big and rich and deep and full makes you happy!

Pranayama teaches us to experience greater awareness of where the external breath seems to dissolve into the atmosphere beyond our physical body. This space of the external breath extends somewhere from 9 to 12 inches beyond the nostrils.

Place your palm slightly in front of your nose. As you exhale, feel your breath on the surface of your palm and gradually move your palm away from your face. (You may be able to feel the breath clearly by moistening your palm.)

How far away can you feel your breath on your palm?

Breathe deeply way down into the belly and feel your spine grow taller. Try it!

Listen to the sweet, sweet sound of your beautiful breath.

Breathe in deep
every possibility...
breathe out and
release every obstacle.

❦ Exhale completely.

❦ Slowly breathe in through the left nostril and softly exhale through the right nostril.
Repeat 3 times.

❦ Then gently breathe in through the right nostril and slowly out through the left nostril.
Repeat 3 times.

❦ Finally, softly and evenly breathe in and out of both nostrils.
Repeat 3 times.

❦ Pause and rest before beginning again.

❦ Repeat for 3 rounds.

inhale as you count to 4
hold as you count to 4
exhale as you count to 4
repeat 3x

continue on if you are comfortable

inhale 6
hold 6
exhale 6
repeat 3x

rest now, or continue on if you are comfortable

inhale 8
hold 8
exhale 8
repeat 3x

rest

Breathe.
Pranayama steadies the mind and
helps you concentrate.
Breathe.

"The single most effective relaxation technique I know is conscious regulation of breath."

~ Dr. Andrew Weil

◨◉◨

Close your eyes and breathe until you experience your true self… luminous, radiant, infinite consciousness.

◨◉◨

"Be in love with existence and let your love be like breathing. Breathe in, breathe out, but let it be love coming in and going out."

~OSHO

Sit or stand in a happy way.
As you inhale sweep your arms as wide as you can and stretch all the way up to the sky.
Flex your palms back as if you are pushing the clouds up high.
Exhale slowly as you stretch your arms long sweeping down along your sides.
Continue and each time take longer, slower smoother breaths and movements.

*B*reathe quietly. Use your inner awareness to find the center of your heart. Feel into it. Breathe into the very center of your heart.

*A*s you inhale, feel the radiant center of your heart grow and expand in all directions. Feel it fill you up. As you exhale, relax and feel the gentle pulsations of your illuminated heart center. Inhale and expand your lustrous, radiant heartspace larger, larger and larger.

*E*xhale and merge into blissful rhythmic pulsations of your heart. Inhale and feel the vibrant rays of your luminous heart shoot out way beyond the stars.

*E*xhale and merge into the cosmos.

◆   ◆   ◆

Conscious breathing is beyond
thought, beyond emotion,
beyond mind.

Try alternate nostril breathing without using your hands. it's simple to do. Lie down and intend to inhale through the left nostril and exhale through the right. Don't use your fingers, simply feel that you are breathing in through the right nostril and out through the left, and then in through the left and out through the right.
Breathe in and out like this for several minutes, then breathe in through both nostrils.

Repeat a few times. You will feel balanced and so very relaxed.

Pranayama is an exalted knowledge.
It is a royal road to prosperity, freedom
and bliss.

~ Yogachidamani Upanishad

✻ Make your spine straight and tall. Breathe. Try your best to breathe with awareness as you sit up tall. Breathing is enhanced when your spine is straight, and your mind is alert. Practice breathing slowly,
deeply and evenly while keeping your spine nice and straight and your mind alert and bright.

Take a deep breath and count to ten.

feel better?

Become aware of your natural breath. Breathe smoothly and evenly and begin to elongate your inhalation and exhalation. Expand your belly and chest as you inhale. Allow your navel to deflate toward your spine as you breathe out.

Keep your face soft and your shoulders relaxed. Be aware of the area in your throat around the throat pit. Gently part your lips and make a soft, long sound as you exhale "haaaaa haaaaaaaa haaaaa".

Now take your palm up to your mouth and exhale as if you were fogging up a mirror. Then close your lips. As you breathe slowly in and out, you will hear a soft, sound — like that of gentle ocean waves, or the sound of a baby breathing. (Some people compare the sound to that of the Darth Vader character in Star Wars.) This is a soothing, soft sound. You should hear it, but not the person on the other side of the room. Continue to slow down and lengthen the breath.

INHALE 4

EXHALE 8

INHALE 5

EXHALE 8

INHALE 6

EXHALE 8

INHALE 7

EXHALE 8

INHALE 8

EXHALE 8

BREATHE NORMALLY.

REST.

Inhale very deeply for one second.
Exhale fully for one second.
Do it for 60 seconds.
Then rest for 60 seconds.

Repeat if you are comfortable.
Inhale very deeply for one second.
Exhale fully for one second.
Do it for 60 seconds.
Then rest for 60 seconds.

If you are comfortable, do it one more time.
Inhale very deeply for one second.
Exhale fully for one second.
Do it for 60 seconds.
Then rest for 60 seconds.

Relax deeply.

Pranayama is perhaps the greatest tool of self-care, the best therapy that we can do for ourselves and without needing to go anywhere, do any exercise or take any drug.

~ Dr. David Frawley

Inhale *SOOOOOOO*
Exhale *HUMMMMM*
~ 108 TIMES ~
40 days in a row

(start over if you skip a day)

Even as the spokes are fastened to the hub, so on this life breath, all is fastened. Life moves with the life breath, which gives life to a living creature. Life breath is one's father, one's mother, one's brother, one's sister and one's teacher.

~ Chandogyopanishad

Conscious breathing purifies your mind.

❤️ INHALE - you are drawing in energy with a natural force of attraction.

❤️ RETAIN your breath after inhalation - you are holding your energy with a force of conservation.

❤️ EXHALE - you are sending energy out with an expressive, electrical force.

❤️ RETAIN your breath after exhalation - you are holding a state of release and expansion.

Practice pranayama every day!

Train your body and your mind to receive the flow of breath. Train your body to be still and train your mind to be still. Breath will help you. Tell your mind to allow your breath to flow naturally in and out. Tell your body to cooperate. Pretty soon, you will only focus on your breath because your body and mind will be in harmony.

Inhale Left ~ Exhale Right

Inhale Right ~ Exhale Left

Inhale Left ~ Exhale Right

Inhale Right ~ Exhale Left

Inhale Left ~ Exhale Right

Inhale Right ~ Exhale Left

Inhale Left ~ Exhale Right

🪷 Rest.

Regulate the breath.
Be happy.
~ T. Krishnamacharya

Breathe into the still timelessness.
Your breath will take you there.
Allow it.

- Sit in a comfortable position.
- Purse your lips like you are going to whistle.
- Focus your eyes on the tip of your nose.
- Inhale through pursed lips.
- Hold comfortably.
- Exhale through the nostrils.

Continue for 10 minutes.

Observe your breath just as you would a beautiful flowing river.

A river of peace.

A river of beauty.

A river of life.

Practice **Breath of Fire** *to remove toxins from your body, bring clarity to your mind, and to bring a rosy glow to your skin.*

❋❋ ❋❋ ❋❋ ❋❋ ❋❋ ❋❋

"When the breath wanders, the mind also is unsteady. But when the breath is calmed, the mind too will be still and the yogi achieves long life. Therefore, one should learn to control the breath."
~Hatha Yoga Pradipika, 14th century CE

❋❋ ❋❋ ❋❋ ❋❋ ❋❋ ❋❋

BREATHE.
JUST BREATHE.

About the Author

Deborah Garland, M.A., E-RYT 500, is a teacher, author and artist in Paradise Valley, AZ where she has taught yoga, pranayama and ayurveda for 20 years. She holds a Master's Degree in Education, is a nationally certified advanced-level yoga instructor and is the founder of Eternal Radiance Yoga, a school for yoga teachers. Deborah's mission is to make pranayama, the practice of yoga breathing, a daily habit for everybody. She trains people from all walks of life - educators, health care providers, yoga teachers and professionals in many fields. Her specialty is helping people make small, easy to manage adjustments in breathing and lifestyle to make very positive shifts in physical, emotional and spiritual wellness. She emphasizes pranayama, yoga, ayurveda, and universal wellness principles. Whether teaching individuals or groups, working with someone affected by ill health, leading a seminar on balanced lifestyle choices, training budding yoga teachers or facilitating pranayama and meditation, her focus is the same: helping people feel and look vibrantly healthy, happy and eternally radiant.

Deborah is available for speaking engagements, workshops and book signings. She would love to hear from you. Contact her at:

www.deborahgarland.com
deb@deborahgarland.com

More from Deborah Garland

Deborah Garland presents a clear, inspiring and practical introduction to pranayama, yoga breathing, to create greater vibrancy and radiance in life.

The yogis mastered the practice of breathing. They understood that breath is both the physical act of respiration and the act of distributing prana. Prana is not only the vital life force, it is also a powerful healing energy in the body that can optimize our physical, mental and emotional well-being.

Supreme Breath, Yogi Breathing to Access Higher Life Force Energy offers easy techniques to reduce stress, slow and reverse the effects of aging, and access your inner source of powerful, radiant life force energy. You will discover age-old yogi secrets and find simple, uplifting and easy to follow methods to develop deeper awareness of your physical, mental and emotional layers, bringing them into perfect harmony. You will discover how to use breathing to feel balanced, healthy and youthful; and learn to handle the ups and downs of life with grace and ease, soon shining with a luminous glow from within.

Check it out! "Supreme Breath" is available on Amazon.com and other online and retail stores. You can also listen to Deborah's voice guiding through the breathing practices! It's available on Audible and iTunes.

Deborah makes pranayama simple, inspiring and approachable for the yogi in all of us!

64048398R00204

Made in the USA
Charleston, SC
20 November 2016